Roberto Clemente

Written by Marcia S. Gresko
Illustrated by Bruce Hedges

Roberto Clemente grew up
in Puerto Rico.
Roberto loved baseball.
He would play ball and
forget to eat.

Roberto went to play baseball in the United States.
Roberto was happy and scared.
He was going far from home.

It was hard to get used to a new place.
Roberto was lonely.
Sometimes he was treated unfairly.

Roberto was a great player.
He hit the ball hard.
He threw it far.
He helped his team to win.
They won the World Series
twice.

Roberto was a kind man.
He taught poor children
to play baseball.
He visited children
who were sick.
He helped new players
on the team.

Roberto cared about
the people who came
to watch him play.

Roberto heard about a bad earthquake.
He got food, clothing, and medicine.
Roberto put everything on a plane.
He went to help.
The plane crashed.

People missed Roberto Clemente. He was a great baseball player and a great man.